Written All Over
Your Face[book]

posted in the year that was 2010
with a little help from my friends

By PMPope

ISBN 978-1-936373-20-8

Published in the United States by Unbound Content, LLC,
Englewood, NJ.
Cover art: Geografistic Stellarium ©2011, by PMPope.
The poems in this collection are all original and previously
unpublished.

Written All Over Your Face[book]

First edition 2011

unbound CONTENT

Dedication

to those without a voice
cast into this world
of noise-some
silence.

to lovers shot down
in rivers of applause
crafted by ravenous crowds.

I pray thee,
keep these words
near & nearer
knowing
you, in my heart,
are always
here & dearer

—PMPope

Table of Contents

Introduction

Reasons for Another {blank}

Anybody can write a book of poetry. Any person possessing the wherewithal to step outside of what is considered profitable and sane should do the world a favor and decide to write all of their innermost thoughts down and make those thoughts dance around to comply with various literary conventions described as poetry. Logical?

The world needs another nameless generic poet/ess like it needs another blog of cool gadgets or a new social networking feature. So why? ... you may ask. Why do we need this book sitting right before us? It's a difficult question to answer. Why should you concern yourself with the literary aspirations of an ex nihilo multimedia poetic artist who has tramped around the country, been clinically deceased, traveled back and forth to Europe {without a dime in his pocket}, performed atrocious acts of performance art, loved more beautiful women than any ugly scoundrel has a right to, survived poverty, hitchhiking, taxi-driving, social barriers, been left for dead, kicked to the curb, left to his own devices ...

Maybe it's more important that the book was written than who has writ it. This book is a collection of literary offerings from the social networks. Social networks have positioned themselves as the key component of modern human interaction. Goodbye salons and coffeeshops! Goodbye bookstores and chance encounters. If we, as a people, prefer the ease and communications of anonymous "untraceable" interaction, it is the communicators' job to adapt to this new form, hence, the artists' virtual studio is now located in the cloud.

Lastly , the world needs love now more than ever. I hope in the publishing of this offering to show that, while not always kind, love should be the constant drive. It solves so many more problems than it creates. While not always easy, its joy spreads better than a spammed trojan virus. This book could not have been actualized without love. I hope that this will inspire the reader to spread it, love, in their own inimitable fashion.

—PMPope

◆————————◆

We only have so many seconds

Do what you can
to not break your own neck
if you step into it
... wipe your shoe
before showing up to the party
where the girls wear their finery
and all the boys from the winery
get polished so they can shine
through the deepest heart of the night
& into the breaking of day

◆————————◆

Definition of Materialized Imagination:
mir-a-cle, noun; any amazing or wonderful occurrence

Friendship

Love Bomb

I grab the trashcan and throw it over a bundle of dynamite. Today is the picnic of our homecoming celebration. This is the last time I will see my friends. To me, the explosion rings into eternity. The metal of the can digs through my chest to embrace my heart.

A Friend of the Animals

Sadie looked at me with her big brown eyes. She wanted to go out. She was crossing her legs and dancing around the living room. It had snowed the night before. I put a little doggie sweater on her and let her out the back door.

Here @the Table

"I'm writing that one down!" exclaims the unflappable barista @the cafe in the University district. I was wondering if I couldn't hold her hand so the line would be sculpted with the original intent. She gigglingly flutters to the other side of the counter. I was wondering if this could be a voyeuristic ... piece of work.

most toxic of all the animals
composed especially for this realm of carbon

I am order #82 @1690 Valencia Street Saturday night
Do you have any idea what this means?
Maybe the entire civilization & social constipation only knows about
smiling rightly
then & there
they sure as heck would like givin' it to you in the ear
simply for the puristic reason
they actually believe that this is the ONLY passage to the brain>> the
heart & subsequently the soul
that most desirous commodity

Birds are going crazy for the weather
for weather is the sole disposition on
the influence of our winged sisters
I wanna fly—high

it's some sort of grubby shell station around here
we keep paying for things with shells
everybody thought there was something screwy about the Indians
buying and selling with beads and feathers
Anyone who is living
is interested in living in Paradise

there are people who live on streets filled with light
there are people who fill life with light
admittedly, these are only two examples
of people types

Here Dolores dips
coming down from 30
with her central divider
with palm tree fingers
tickling the belly
of the cool night sky
flicking off
a couple airplanes & satellites

Here i am with her
cresting the 26th Street summit
without jogging gear, wheels, wings or any standard commodity
to show for my life's work up 'til now.

There is a palm frond in the middle of the crosswalk
@Caesar Chavez & Dolores
I drag it & drop it on my path up this climb
Here is 26th crested with her hills all jeweled out

the Architect of the Cosmos
taps me on the shoulder
& "Vannas" the hills all around & sez to me alone at the top
"There is beauty in the things humans do."
so ... there is beauty in the things we do?
"Yes."
Agreed. There is beauty in these things we do.
We are capable of doing beautiful things.
"Yes."
Again with the "Yes."

It is my privilege to walk upon this planet
'though times the elements rush cold & harsh
or may even force the chill
spooky rattle of scaffolding plastic
Viola! I can see her from here
the corner of Church & Liberty
She beckons me back to the center of the City
@night
into the flux
of the fluttering flicker
Light of her wings

In History as in the Air

Return the machine to its factory settings
Little girls love furry animals
There's no kind of business, I know
... Quite like the roar & the smoked mirrored frame
And all the clever boys
Plying their clever trades
If you'd close your eyes to the screen
Maybe you'd hear the blood-curdling scream
Of a director calling
"Quiet on the set!"

◆————————————————◆

Visions @Earthtime

Call me out into the ether
Today is a good day to fly
Tie a feather to my wrist
... I hold your hand with fingertips
In velvet space the cosmic wraps our gaze
You & I slide into the eye
Captured timeless in celestial frame

◆————————————————◆

———◆———

When You Breathe

Take a little bit in through your nose
the fragrance of life
smell the world
... it is politics & action
smell the trees growing
warm summer spice
of muscadine & radish
smell the stars moving the sky
subtle in the distant
love waits patient
for the next gentle day

———◆———

Attach

Attach something personal
to your heart for me
a piece of cloth
... once used to draw back your locks
as we ran from the storm clouds
through unending fields of prairie flowers
months of carnivals rolling through the plains
drawn in migration
toward a glittering
cornsilk smile

The MEPIS/Clock Conundrum

Flotsam ...
Maybe that IS the key
Speculating @the pier
w/ a beer
Hoping for the underlying
understanding
of what could possibly be amiss
Somewhere
in the file system &/or OS
OS
OS
OH
OS
How the navigators signal
SOS
'Twasn't the beer which read
that which Debian Girl writ
'Fore MEPIS was download
burned to a disc
Applied & re-tried
only as far as an hour & one quarter
of peacefully tense walltime
"Oh MEPIS, Oh MEPIS ...
Memtest ...
Eighty-six
Oh MEPIS, Oh MEPIS ...
Memtest ...
Eighty-six,"
et al ...
"Get outta there, man!
How many passes do you do?"
Hit the magic ESC
Boot it back into Etch 4.0 screen
"Computer ... what could the damage be?"
I've traveled two hours into the future
or so it would seem
from timezone PST

BUT!
When I gaze toward the little clock
from Walgreen's
I learn I have not gained two hours
INDEED
I click on the little clock
which I placed
at the top of the start screen
only to find myself
with my limited knowledge
unable to effect a "real" time change
so back to work
and/or back to the pier
my mind on the flotsam
the clock
and the gears ...
OS
OS
OH
SOS
I guess

—————◆—————

Solitude on a Payment Plan

Get it
While you still have time
There's no reason to rush
You could make your head spin
By doing something more clever
Think: selling your plasma
To lower your cholesterol
So you'll have a few more hours
To show some love

◆—————◆

Light Has Come to Time

Clock face sweeping
wipe the hours from the dust
Meteoric in expanse
rippling through celestial curtain
Take a picture
it'll last longer
kiss upon inviting lips
all your life will never lose
will always linger
will never leave

———◆———————————◆———

Squeezing Out the Remaining Drops

She would watch while sleeping
movements on the surface of the Moon
In her "day-to-day"
She'd mimic going through the motions
pushing LED time with a mind full of expectation
of what could & should be
when closed the eyes
diving into a pool of dream

———◆———————————◆———

In Response to Perspective

Perspective as sticky as pasta noodles
where the late-night wonderkin show up
for a bit of the yodel-lay-ee-o in unregistered vehicles
from quadrant L7 of the Vortox Galaxy ...
But for my stretched-out grasshoppers I'd be soRely aMiSS.
"An opinion does not a truth make" ... I made that up, I think.
I looked it up on Google and it can't be attributed to anyone I can find.
So ... if no one can prove me wrong, I'm claiming that quote as my own.
theory rules the airwaves ... scientific method went out the door in 1984
I'd rather be doin' this than Facebookin' in some stuffy igloo
in the shadow of an oil farm
with Mongolians & Russians playing poker for my knucklebones.
there is, however, something very special about
stayin' in a Yurt in mongolia ...
drinkin' horse milk,
chasin' that steppe muse ...
sublime infinite!

◆————————————◆

Cyber-shadow Wonder

new catalogs of criticism have arrived from far away
lady loves the leaves from the tree disentangled
themselves for a portion of the evening or season in the sun
when a drunken driveler decides to dribble aloud
"Hereforth whereth ye roam"
like while waiting for something much more attractive
or copping a feel in the darkest recess of cyberspace

◆————————————◆

◆———————————◆

Testing the Pink of Lips

Her anything
which would strap me to this sleep forsaken machine loop
longer than a sock stuck on spin
if it weren't for the memory
of a long remember'd kiss
o' stars in a cycle of Moon
chase Sun image stuck in synaptic skipping groove ...
stuck in these synap ...
skipping ...
sticky skynaptic g ...
rooves of well-tasted
electric pink
psi shell full
this cosmic nerve
rock
kiss

◆———————————◆

Fan Mail

GOTTA KEEP DAT PRIV BRA ... I AM YER BIGGEST FAN OF YER PRESIENT POETRY ... DO NOT ... I REPEAT ... DO NOT POST ANY MORE DRUNKEN DRIVEL ... YER BETTER THAN THAT ... A BRO POET SPEAKS TO U ... WHEN SHE SMILES>ROSE PINK>AHHHHH! MY FAVORITE PERFUME!

you're funny ... If I had drunk it might've been more professional!Ha! No ... I've got those: "trying-to-stick-250-words-into-a-142-character-limit" Blues. Keep the peace.

Mysterions of Time Stop By for A Visit

The corvids have returned to the deck of my ship
Carrying in their beaks twigs of reconstituted fettucine
And strings of magnetic ribbon data files ...
Though no land has been spotted through the last forty years
Of this lonely voyage
I feel a brand new day

—◆————————◆—

Say Brother Wind & Sister Rain

give a little
all you have
to those around you
you can see
give a little more
from what you keep
for yourself
blow the clouds
grow the flowers

◆————————◆—

Reality has come to us all.
It is the dawning of a new day.
Eradicate the shadows of darkness.
Shine the light on everything.
Let Love Live!

—————————◆

Braid of Stars {to be worn}

Let me twist a braid of stars
into a ribbon for you
It isn't the hardness of a diamond you are
...veins of silver are weened of poison scars
if you'd drop that cruel armor
wrapped around the fragile heart
lose yourself to the crush of my arms
i would pull down a curtain of stardust
wrap you in this vision
watch you shimmer spectral
in the copper crystal of my love

◆—————————◆

Nobody Likes Palindromes Anyway

Trying hard to play the doctor
"I've got the cure you've been dreaming of ... "
but ... damn, y'all
making it hard for a colored man
to walk among the birds
not that i'm an afro samurai
throw the glitter in the air
wait for it to turn on a dime
into heart bent morphere
wishing on a fallen start
on a starlit saturday night

Palindromatic 10-20-2010

Yawn a more Roman way
Yo banana boy!
Yo bozo boy!
...Won't I panic in a pit now?
Won't lovers revolt now?
Salt an atlas
Otto sees Otto
Otto made Ned a motto
Madam, in Eden I'm Adam
Ma has a ham
Ma is as selfless as I am
Decaf and DNA faced
We few
We panic in a pew
UFO tofu
So many dynamos

◆————————————◆

Delight in the Out of Sight

I'd brush my fingers
down your cheek
along the petulance of your chin
were my fingers as reaching
as an ocean
which long ago
caressed the face
of the glacier as she ran
across the chromatic plains
for once to take a chance to brush
a single sound
a solar sigh
falling from your parted lips

◆————————————◆

Dust the Yoke
{for the children & animals of the new workforce}

In those days of days before their fogs were completely known,
the ox and the child
worked one with the other
new sparkler in water lawns
sunrise erected each morning

Before those mosquito planes
sent back their first intrepid {Ibex}
wave of technology
non-nightvision ultrasound images
of this *new* day
first seagull in the airshaft
its first hour laughed
its first laugh of this or any other morning

This eyelid is pried
from Sleep's sticky sweet
dream realm he beckons the sent
into this stew of living mess
angry sounding life
car and construction
cable and scremas
of\sirens\
miserables\constantly

recognition engaged
the books are all here
hoo raa!
another day without accumulation
of life threatening bullet holes
or more Love than
granted in once non-distant dream

Those days of lucid dreaming certifiably fresh
in my mien
Recently Accessible Memory
children don't NEED these. Everything from the past is
taboo
and wrinkled
and expires
on the day they were born.

In my ox mask, I wait,
in the rain, in the heat, in the noise,
on my feet ... until my strength is
once again necessary ...
Ring-a-ding!
A bell in phones' plastic housing
beats "You stupid lummox! Why don't you
pick up the phone?"
as stated before
the ox is the mask
to which
this goat applies itself well
& waiting is working
as New Times do tell ...

———◆———————————◆———

Raphael

In the season of ghouls, isn't it nice to know your pets are protected from evil?
In this episode of the Weekly Crow! Calendar, we see Rocky get a spritzing
from the local Franciscan
priests during a Blessing of the Animals ritual, during the Feast of St. Francis.
Hope you enjoy this hi-speed
calendar and get out and show love to all your neighbors! Peace!
Raphael is the Angel of Marriage, of Healing, of Happy Meetings, of Travel & of
Joy!
How do I know?
"For I am the angel Raphael, one of the seven who stand before the Lord."

—Tobias 12:15

◆———————————◆

Direct Communication

Prayers to Arch-Angel
Raphael is the guardian
of marriage
of healing
of happy meetings
of joy & of travel
That's direct communication with the Ultimate
Power of the Multiverse
who knows all the suffering
carting down here
We could wrap all the hearts of the world
if we wished
in a Carolina sky blue ribbon
around the ponytail
of a laughing girl child
in fields washed with gold

Crossing Across Space

I've nothing for you
Take my empty hand
No boots
No dresses
No beauty parlor visits
No foreign money orders
No running through the airports
No crowded photographs
No long lost embrace
I'm wearing no sleeves
No sack on my back
Working in the chimney
Covered in soot
I've only a heart pumping blood
A brain for collecting image
A tongue to taste
Sweet words of the lips
And eyes
To capture the light
Of your heart
And the warmth of you
Love
Which is more than enough for me
Enough for any man
To live out his days
Thousands of miles of railroad tracks
Away from the epicenter
Of your garden
How the garden swells
In the spring
What wondrous
Gifts the gentle rains bring
The music of the spheres
The trumpets of bees
While worlds away
You and me
Gaze deeply
Hand to hand

I'm Not From Around Here

If tomorrow you are offered
a gift beyond value
without tags attached
from the hand outstretched
given freely with knowing
no such gifts exist as such

If the next day the entire curtain is lowered
all the seahorses are released from their bowls
all the prisoners set free, the blind to see
cripple and lame are dancing in the street
the noise of life stifled by the gentlest sigh

The news services declare
all poverty, crime & murder have vanished
into the thinnest of the purest air
no hatred for money
no hatred of race

I pray thee, beloved,
remember thou me
for such an otherworldly spectacle
is that for which I arrived
and that for which

———◆—————————◆———

Thank You, Jeff Buckley!

Reminds me of Amsterdam as I strode out one morning!
"Love is not a victory march/it's a cold & it's a broken hallelujah!"
I remember thinking: that's almost too sharp inside the heart.

———◆—————————◆———

———◆————————————◆———

Love Simply Conquers All

Don't get too smart to out think the Universe
or the Multiverse may step on your head
if she would give,
i would receive
no matter how dorky it would seem
to the clever children
or the washed out & shipwrecked geriatrics
if you have nothing else to give
why not consider
Love
?

◆————————————◆

Today Is a Polka Dot Pudding

Connect the dots even if it
won't earn you a jot
from
-the self styled
-the buzz merchants
-the anti-aunties
ripple & roll that butterfly wing
grab that chicken & start to sing
wing in wing
"We are free!"

◆————————————◆

Awake the Mind of the Heart

Dr. Google can't fix a samurai heart
after the airport vultures
have made their mark

◆————————————◆

One Petal Falls @24fps

I look to the sky until I can't look any further
I look to the sky and pray for my brothers
It used to be about dimes
Now it's much further
Stakes are high
Now it's about quarters
We were raised by grandmothers
Now we're barely raised by mothers
No loyalty, no morals
No hard work and pain
All it's about
Fun and games
Let's get it together
Time waits for no man

———◆———

Love Everyone; All the Time

There is none to be unloved
Love your enemies & mine
with the same ferocity ...
Love is the only change
to change the hearts
of those who would orchestrate your demise
that is worth all the riches
this world has to offer
try it TODAY!
it's never too late
to let love in
to let love win

———◆———

———————

Offered for Your Edification

I often find difficulties
in attempting to "place"
my writing with magazines &
publishers.
This is one example.
It is a six-page poem.
It contains factual incidents
as well as the "freeverse,"
lyric, and phrase
enjoyed as the poetic "meat & potatoes"
from the modern poets.
{re: post-50s/60s}. I hope
you ... will enjoy this piece
and contact me directly if
you can think of something
I have neglected in
this offering.
Pace e bene.

———————

———◆————————————◆———

Time Travel While Holding Hands

It can be cold in this world
Some of the imagery comes from years
focal length can tell us only so much ...
but flying, man, we love it as our form
of constant communication
we talk to the wind
about the stars & the prism
we share words
on the breath
of a dreaming kiss

———◆————————————◆———

———◆————————◆———

Roostering it up, as it were

That 10-10-10 thing was mind altering
Today is not another day
First things first ...
Making waffles & soysages
To absorb the muscadine & grape
from a reeling through the fractalverse
Frankenstein it all together
& calendar up the "Crow!"

———◆————————◆———

◆————————————————◆

Tea Party Saturday Night

Changes we can't possibly realize are occurring at each moment. Let LOVE in!
The Light changes position. The water changes density. The Earth changes size &
shape. I must allow myself to change into a form acceptant of change. Pace e luz.

Today's is the Last 10-10-10 for a thousand years
October 10 at 7:54pm

Art produced as artists discussed spiritual matters.
Sounds like another Saturday night around the Haywire Manor.

These all stem from a conversation with an etheric spirit
as we drank tea on opposite sides of the world
Pace e lux

◆————————————————◆

————◆————

Invi-divisable

In public -
UNnoticed -
it is quite possible to fall
through the
groove -
the pattern UN
recognized - in the
TEXT
ured tread of {her} books

————◆————

◆———————————————◆

Are You Going to Be There?

All the birds sing
& dance through the morning sky
Starbeams translate into sunshine
Earth's flesh longs for the touch
of the inexplicably divine
Clear? I'm clear?
to any which one to decide
"Come to the feast"
rolls across the piedmont hills
for all to choose
accept or decline

◆———————————————◆

Physical Illusion of Sensation

Rockets red glare y'all
glared through the hair
covering the flesh
wrapped in the bone skull
directly connected
through a young human's
still developing cerebellum,
similar reaction, it is,
{i have this upon
my very best authority},
to that of a plastic arrow
with a cheap little tin head
sticks through the tendons
of the elbow
a fearless finger reaches ...
curious to touch near
the incisive entry point,
a fearless finger reaches
the spot
to know,
how does it feel?
eyes & brain disagree
It's some other couple
millimeters away
People go to sleep as such
& their kids, too.
They wish they had bikinis
rather than snowshoes
stitched up in silicon designer
boutiques for bored, restless, techni-kiddies
spending their electric salamander days
impressing large women with
roadmap hands & also the insanely thin
marching pink, tan, obsidian, bronze,
and white.
The very edifice of this city, these hummingbirds
darting through ivy draped on the trellises,
which is expected more than anticipated
during these high days of Spring.

The human eye takes really,
really bad single cell freeze
frame photography.
Esp. for the avant worker
plying Plato mosques
in pedestrian malls of the uber palms
discussing start-ups dissing
the bold & innovative
better hope her daddy foots
the bill or the proprietary drivers
of their software empire may
crumble just like split ends
& ten dollar bills for manicures
from Little Saigon ...

Clocktower, swing your arms
all around your face
filled with carbohydrates
& your Monday thru Friday skirts
hanging in the entryway
for easy access
& comfortable & mellow & friendly
are all "made-up" qualities
no one would rather possess or
find themselves in possession of

@1:30 the starling waiters come to clean the tables
as the starving beggars head for the cans
it's not too shocking for you to consider
when you think about the way we treat those fellows.
Better it should happen here, i guess, than some alien planet
on the dark side of the moon or underneath the raging overpasses of
defunct & non-funded off ramp construction where the tribes
of primates star in their own reality network programming
& everyday
& every hour
it's surviving idols are lost in Time & in Space

Alchemical Manifestation w Flowers & Ice

Heat ... humid ... ice melt
Me @metal cafe
Ant running across iron grate
Of hair & amp; time on my arms
Condensation beading plastic
Clouds fill bowl of sky
Oh, that it were proper
Sew up the blue splotches
With all this silver gray along the line
We could then pretend they'd never been
Even if it were revealed through us
Via these lenses less glamourized;
Less memorized
Than through utility
Of memorial or sensationalism
Harvested @one of dem
Lyrical financial academies
Even if one of our dearest,
Lovely, darling poet/ess/e/s
Took a portrait of crimson petals
Yawning @the gate of the State pen
Out in Pennsylvania {You Got a Friend}
Where the hearts of the hardened
Concrete convicts crumble
& amp; all the while
Ice melts in plastic
@a metal cafe

Untitled

You don't know me
not because you wouldn't like to
more likely, i am a bit too off-setting for the casual readers,
who're used to popping caustic scenes of pop
culture down their respective & communal gullet,
at a break neck pace,
relishing all the gusto they could muster.
Man, they'd throw those things down
like a big ol' greasy bag of Warholian Plaster Chips,
if the media moguls would manufacture them
out where the bullets shine
at a USA plant attached to a fireworks speakeasy.
Drug dealers, gang bangers, one-legged albino hooker midgets ...
everyone gets the spotlight for what the market makes ...
truth & beauty are the ugliest fish in the barrel ...
gee, ain't it funny how pretty
strength is formed outside
& internal fortitude from an entirely other place?
I don't want you thinking I haven't loved
every subtle nuance we have ever shared.
I would like you to pick up all this trash
you've scattered around my living space
& do us all the favor of building your altar, to your fallen idols ...
elsewhere ...
like ...
far, far away.

Rise & Shine, All You Hearts

People everyday
Grab the things that matter
Try to be a force for loveliness
send out positive vibrations
towards all the creatures
towards all the nations
no matter their features
they are all created in loveliness
all created for Earthly matter
everyday people
People everyday

◆────────────────◆

I never said it would be a walk in the park

Yesterday was a day just like any other. The sky: blue. Sun held stationary in a perceptual and fixed point overhead. You'd think one would be immune from the feeling of "defeat" simply by willing it to be so ...

◆────────────────◆

◆————————————————◆

Ugly

Not much you could do to make it look any better
Sell it to the cataract encrusted masses
I lose a little bit more each & every day
I don't have to
consult the dictionary
for the definition of: Death Warmed Over
that's what mirrors are for

◆————————————————◆

———————◆———————

Our Most Beautiful Lady of Poverty

We are drawn to your warmth
the love
which knows no exclusivity
Naked we entered this dance
leave it we shall
as the tune draws down
little do we obtain
that has not been given
in the brilliant sunshine glow
of this translucent splendor
you bestow

—*In honor of St. Francis of Assisi*

———————◆———————

◆—————————◆

Blessing the Pet

Fur, four-legs, fins, & feline flickering tails
Life's culture is on parade
for your love & consideration
all animals are animals
no matter the breed
what is needed to succeed
is the sharing & the caring
of small moments together
—in tribute to our animal companions

◆—————————◆

Glass of Drink Liquid

Need something to slake this scratch
eyes itching in the sockets
every time I venture outside this cocoon
Blinded, i become
with lovely piercing beams
of angles & curves
& texture & color
walking as dreams walk
through autumn fragrances
of wood & flesh

———◆———————————◆———

Enough for us

Reach into the further out
with forefinger & thumb
grab a kernel of the fruit of the wheat
rub it between your palms
scent of grass can fill your nose
with the sound of something sweet

———◆———————————◆———

Compostable Crank Handles

Elevators can be capricious especially
when scented with wilted licorice

Machines could be out to getcha
—PLEASE IGNORE THAT—

Sing praise
of self interested masses, all your friends,

the most friended, washout cinema scars,
& heroes tasting wine @$uper discounts

fingering alien devices
you get gold stars for figuring out
which somehow'll equate to MPG
squared to the N
equation of nuclear family

spindling so barely binary
Gee, that's lucky
you're so clever

Say:
a doctor
needs
a doctor

whoever
you treat
in whichever
way
This is
the way
YOU
will be
treated

If you think you could afford it, howzabout spend some love,
on somebody who needs it
there are lots of us heading off into "good night."
without the imprint of lips &/or warmth to keep us moving on

———◆———

Philip Pope Thinks

Philip Pope thinks "the obvious" needs to go home and get ready for
2morrow in order that WE
{its customers} recognize it & cheer as it struts down the sidewalks
—Loud the World is—
blasting peace from memory/is love loud?
Moving forward using all that's left/
making love to you with every measured step/
ordinary was never/
our state of grace

———◆———

◆————————————◆

Shout for Joy!

Wrinkled winds blow through crumpled landscapes
Overcast skies herald dawn's next gift
Angels set up camp alongside the creekside
I could sell it to the world
with the proper F-stop
as long as love
would every morn
rise & shout
its song to me

◆————————————◆

What Wynter Leaves {fin}

Always falling for stuttering girls
as they stumble
& gambol
& frolic
the coffee doesn't do the whole thing that needs to be done
{@least once, before one's scheduled departure from this cube of existence}
"Please ... hold on."
stalling hesitation on crunchy earthen wings
18 to 80 blind, crippled & crazy
" ... you can't realize what you are looking @
until it has been explained to you."
la primera tiempo
is there anything different about the smell of early Spring nights?
Not in this city, but, you know, Oaktaown gets a fresh blast of sunset in its face ...
hard to say anything with certainty
except for transparent things you can see
these you experience on the way out through the financial district dow ... N
into the Eastern facing piers ...
new world of flavors
filled with shapes
smothered in multi-tiered sound ...
sports fans go wild
seagulls are barking their approval
of what it is that is going down
turns into a long, long weekend
herefore, the temperature drops another couple of inconsequential degrees
fortunately for the unfortunates
these are some things that have been brought over here on this side of the Bay
where it keeps on balancing out ofttimes you may catch yourself
deep, deep in the red ...
that's
just another part of the whirly-gig cosmic fractal
so don't freak out ... manufactured lifeforms!

Online newscurl from the info allies
the last one was shot in the northern regions of Spain.
Luckily for the webheads the scientifically minded were on the ball
{enough @least} to throw the very last traces of DNA into
the deep freeze & inject that very same frozen Ibex stuff
into your run-of-the-mill she-goat ovum
You simply must jump up
onto the back of the Ibex
ride that wild goat
it eats what it sees
smells it with Love
worships it sacred
knowing only what it knows
not an enemy
a breeze through the trees
up the mountainside
without flanneled criminal elitism
it races the season's approach through the valley
past the home on the range free to be @total liberty

———◆———

Silver Day, She Rolls

Down the slope she strides with an easy gait
taking in changes erupting monochromatic
with the verdant as vibrant
as any sweet sprig of spring's eternal emerald
now she paints it chrome silver
singing its jangly folkloric lyric
reserved for blindingly blue days
next to approach will be the white
cold beard scrounging through the bricks
during festivals of blood and wine

———◆———

◆————————————————◆

Some Lovely Memory Stuck

There was a time to think you could've
Gone that extra mile to the fair
Away down the frozen aisles

Between the river and the field
For the flair to sport
I couldn't think of one thing finer
Than your watery gold dripping
Through my fingers

A night so capped with yearning for the next
Atop a sunken ship
So full of stars & stops

◆————————————————◆

Translucent Kind

Looking through is quite the thing to do,
or so t'would seem to anyone who was born on this planet
in the last hundred years or so. Look through the leaves
of black and white newsprint and you may find something
to pique your interest. Glass comes to mind
as an elegant solution to increase your chances
of looking through something without causing much of a fuss.
The great thing about looking through
glass is that it forms a physical barrier to an other dimension which
you could, if you so desired, become an object within and in doing so
change your entire reality. Look through the lenses
of glasses or cameras. You'll notice three versions of time
occurring simultaneously. Look through a magazine or a deck
of cards, your imagination will soar with all sorts of possibilities.
Look deep into the eyes of your pet. You may unlock the very mysteries
of the soul. Looking through your list of friends
may give you an indication of who you are
and what you hope to archive in this life.
Take a long, deep look.

Mindful of This Never Forgotten Day {9-11}

There was a day when we were called
attention was captured
united collectively
froze welded into a people's being

This series of tragedies occurred
not because of any of us, individually
but who we are, were, and will be
will ever draw the ire
from the fuse of the fire
lit by the fingers of hate
and fearful of greed & jealousy

Mothers began the wail
raised into the heavens
on pillars of smoke

Brothers and sisters stopped
dead in their tracks
for lack of belief

Fathers, feeling powerless to explain
began planning a rescue
of all that were left

There will be a day
when the smoke will dissipate
the rains will come
all that is broken
will be swept away
even of memory
there will be a day

———————————————

Hear the pounding

Weavers on their looms
a-looming the luminous
clack! the wood replaced with steel
songs of future men repeal
Let's get histrionic & historically sardonic
for a year and a day
sew the fabric off your rack
roll, baby, roll ... feel the sweat, give it slack
of good, honest, hard-earned pull
of goodly honest working pay
Cash it in
kick the tires
pray that love will light the way

———————————————

———◆———————————————◆———

Distance Between Heaven & Earth—for the traveler

One step separates the East from the West
one slice of banana in Elvis' Peanut Butter sandwich
One cherry & two lemons
one well placed device to disrupt the organic flow
One girl in a yellow fisherman's raincoat
one flash of inspiration etched into a photograph
One kiss from the day before yesterday

———◆———————————————◆———

Lucky to be Stimulaic
{for the girls forgetful of breathing}

There is no superstition. Only the bill,
the price of the bill,
and ability to pay what is mistaken for the balance ...

Everybuddee! With fist raised, pumping overhead
displace non-visible molecules
Orange walls catch everything

A child swaddled in the trappings
of a far flung solar flare
ignites as it strikes a palm tree pose
betwixt stainless gears
of soul

Shrink wrap reactionaries spread open arms across
sunrise ...

The only rooster
in the air shaft
sighs loudly, full of rustic spunk
"It is here! It is here!
I will do my job
to all these modern chickens!"

This echoed threat falls on the skewered earlobes of ghettopunk
deciding to punt the puny pups weaned from their bitch nipples
'cause mama whimpered fearful
arms loaded full of animated sundials, plastic magnet thermometers,
hypodermic databases of electrocuted alkaline, battery of bullets
{with every preacher's name laser etched
into their proprietary casings}
accompanied by the weeks-old stenchings of sweat
left
lightyears & increments,
& seconds of Aeons
ago

i'm tired.
i want to be away from the animals.
2morrow i have to get up:
strangle that rooster
protest against non-cruelty free products & those luddite businesses
employing them
write an electron-
ic letter to a virtual girl
interact with numbers on a screen
pray for heaven to fall on me
pay some taxes to the bankrupt
look for food to eat

flesh and bone du jour:
gold
gas
guns
& guts

Those crazy SF girls believe
Friday the 13th
more than February 14th
that's twisted & perverse.
what sort of person could they be hoping to sleep with? Are You
attracted to creatures like this?

gush while you can
Gravity washes gravy
down
dope sick drains
everything would be perfect
but:

#1—my legs itch
{solipsistic reaction
{i hope}
}
#2—i have no kitchen
or toilet
to call my own,
anytime i want, i can't
walk barefoot into ceramic
fists on hips
admire the porcelain
"That's where I do my business.
Me ...
& those I allow!"
not a chance
to pull open the airtight door seal
gaze across the well lit food products
{in various stages of consumability}
before smug bougie blurgation
"Leftovers!"

Today is the holiday of misappropriation and false assumptions

i have none
to share these with here
regardless
only faded glories
dreams of the future
mnemonic media of past archivistic intention

Amy receives a Saint Valentine's Day cookie from the O'Farrell Street Boudin.
She works @Walgreen's
She could care ... Not to ...
meet the Guinness Girls @coated posters saying inside Kennedy's ... Join us!
"Good guys," or as Sal calls the Steinbeckian couple smoking our grotto
and making a sign of the cross ... "this man never down," walking down the beach
through the rolling spumes of all
these 18 to 30 year old kids
celebrating

Antigua New Years Eve ... And I'm like swimming under water ...
I've never seen a mushroom in my life ... Gloria! Gloria! In Excelsis Deo!
Don't think for a second the finger is not measuring the pulse ...
Not one second the eye is separate from the synaptic brain ...
Not one number connected neural ... Nor one shoebox in Reno
where they're not praying for a box of whiskey to publish shows for all ages ...
MEANWHILE ... Back @the Morlock ... Bren & I were making up stories ...
about Mothers and adventures ... well past the time of the most recent
bailout package of stimulus
{that's Happy Hour, kids}

Screen Drain

my brain is melting from lack of stimulus or maybe too much of the wrong stimulus. I feel my life force is being drained for no other reason than I am spending every waking hour watching one screen or another.

——————◆——————

The Passing Crowd

Watch & learn
How to be a good little human
Who breaks the laws
Who pays the bills
Who sucks it up
Who hurts from lonely

——————◆——————

Chiefly Concerned With the Absence of Love
{as the world winds down}

Her arms were never so strong
as the advertisement made them out to be
Holding nothing in her arms
she seems slightly softened
The advertisement should have made that point
as a disclaimer
"Objects are closer than they appear"
Or, at least, "Objects appear closer than they should"
Or you could really bust their chops
If the advertising dollar was spent
on the idea of simplicity for simplicity's sake
Then Rosie the Riveter may somehow've lived
an honest and unassuming life
In a little cottage in New Jersey
without being an icon
Of a schematic device used profusely
to build tensions into whatever political potpourri
The kids find jangling in their pockets
as they head off into their targeting rages

Space Junk and the Inevitability of Catch Up

When your hair is bouncing in the breeze
You'd never think to see
Head held back to stare at the sky
Look up there!
That cloud looks like a tombstone
Yet on closer inspection
Hurtling from the atmosphere
Old space junk satellites
How was it when in the 70s we first heard Lou Reed
Sing of Satellites of Love
But today no one could believe how all the junkies
With their canes and their permanent
Game Over! Mental codecs
Shuffle through the E. Village and Alphabet City
So much discarded refuse
That broke our hearts & now the rain of space junk
Is reported by new crews
While smiling and reminding us:
If you see space debris
Call the police immediately.
After all,
It is government property.

———◆———————————◆———

Finalize the Project

Time is not what the world says it is
it is a helper
a lover of quality
a bringer of seasons
a granter of insight
& also,
the only way
the spiritually bankrupt
can justify their existence

———◆———————————◆———

—◆————————◆—

When I See Your Picture in My Head

All i can say that i think i thought i knew
was the time we were one in the moonlight
burning with the plasma of a tear
& our song filled every bird of the air
with flight
with joyous delight & luxurious grace
that time grants to be savored in the hindsight
of a lonely broken vacant space
from as much as i can tell tonight

—◆————————◆—

◆————————————————◆

Transparencies Covering Years

If you have ever felt you were too old or too young
to be taken seriously by the whose-a-what's-its
Carve the finest niche into your heart's deepest recess
store the knowledge of that emotion
in the crawlspace full of boxes;
the boxes full of pictures;
the pictures drawn in crayon;
colored with magic markers;
& ribbons stuck with glitter & glue

—For Diana Marie on her birthday

◆————————————————◆

———◆————————————◆———

Dental Hi-Jinx

With an Envelope from my estranged father of forty-four years lying next to a plastic bag of cables & power chords, I consider the shark.

Today the teeth aren't too bad. Mine usually orchestrate a symphony of pain. I have the teeth of a shark. They aren't connected to the jawbone. They float in the gums and bump against... the bone decay. I tried once to bite a girlfriend on the back pocket of her jeans. Holy mama! that was my first experience of the extreme dental hell-pain I would find myself thrust into throughout my adult life.

———◆————————————◆———

————————◆

Tragic for Living Hearts

We must expect, @the time when we burn our little sparks
This is a fleeting theater of organic cloth
we look into the sky not knowing
the express passage of seconds
ticking through living hearts.

————————◆

———◆———◆———

Chrome Day to the Healers

Pain has been raging across the bone forest
Now with the Sun does it subside
Love has been calling
to hear your voice dearest
Precious the touch
lovers & healers apply

———◆———◆———

———————◆

Your Pain I Feel

Pain for me
Pain for you
sometimes it seems
just for me
or just for you
let's not forget
we are in this together
even though worlds away
pain for me
is
pain for you

———————◆

In Need of Muse Things

smell of flower on cool night
touch of milk & silk of skin
relieve this pain
of being man

Hemp Piece

Hemp for health
Hemp for hope
Hemp for homes
Hemp for humans
What part of this aren't you getting?
Hemp for horticulture
Hemp for healing
Hemp for houses
Hemp based vanilla milkshakes
Just chime in when you catch a whiff
Hemp brewed beer
Hemp infused hotcakes
Hemp for homeless hound dogs
Hemp for happiness
Hemp for erectile dysfunction
Hemp for the holidays
Hemp for Honda
Hemp for Hundavi
It burns really clean, dude
Hemp for heating
Hemp for hippies
Hemp for high falutin' hillbillies
Hemp flavored hot dogs
Hemp based high dollar handshakes
It's got, literally, over a million-plus uses
Messengers of Hemp
Industrialization of Hemp
Space shuttles built with and powered by
Pilots powered by Hemp
Diplomas of Hemp
The amazing world of Hemp
Chickens & pigs raised on Hemp
{Prophetic Hemp visions of green eggs and ham}

Chill out on a rug made of Hemp
High tech chips of Hemp
A spot of tea brewed Hemp
A reliable broom built with Hemp
Biodegradable plastics of Hemp
3rd quarter increases in the production of Hemp
A "Get-Out-of-Jail-Free" card printed with soy based ink
On 15-lb stock of Hemp
The Dunder Mifflin of Hemp
The Levis of Hemp
Musical instruments of Hemp
Farming hats of Hemp
Gardening gloves of Hemp
Scarecrows stuffed with Hemp
American flags of Hemp
High octane hot rods fueled with Hemp
Pictures of George Washington in a field of Hemp
Woodstock's got nothing on Hempstock
Reduction in crime caused by Hemp
Reduction in suffering caused by Hemp
Reduction in poverty caused by Hemp
Reduction in unemployment caused by Hemp
Reduction in the negative side effects of pharma-based society
Caused by Hemp
Increase in American production caused by Hemp
Increase in farming based lifestyle caused by Hemp
Increase in future stock trading caused by Hemp
Increase in appreciation of nature caused by Hemp
Increase of peace and spirituality caused by Hemp
Increase of philosophical debate caused by Hemp

God Almighty, thank you for all this Hemp
Earth sustains us with Hemp
The sunrise reminds us of Hemp
The sunset is brilliantly Hemped
Through the forest and woodland glade
off we go a-Hemping
Evaluate the Hemp
Re-evaluate the Hemp
Grow, grow, grow Hemp
Think about what you've got—Hemp
Don't chase after someone else's crop—Hemp
Jump up on the harvest wagon—Hemp
Let's buy American Hemp
Our Hemp is of high quality
Excelsior, Hemp!
You have saved our economy
From total and humiliating collapse
Run on a Hemp platform
Into a Hemp frontier
Hemp men & Hemp women
UNITE! For this truly is
to be
Hemp's finest hour!

Resizing Our Partitions

Remember way, way back?
pert' damnear goin' on ...
a half a disk of gigs ago
you held it in your hand
tender & secure
cooing you said
like a little bird
Unsheathing that broadside
bound in treacherous foil
blue now gray with compost-
ible passage of hourly years
feverish with fat baby glee
tu guitarra es abrir ...Abrir!
Guardia Alta for Manciolino's
Primo Assalto
unleashing a flamenco mariachi
in the midst
of this politically incorrect
{sorry, that should be "PC"}
Zarzuela
—that's at least three different things going on
at one time—
Who could hope
to wait
to love?
All the poets are dead.
Their alien winds obliterate
sweeping decades of history
for pennies a day
children sit
drooling into screens
people are dying of thirst
without one cool drop
on their lips

Blind Architect

the roof is tiled
with solar paneling
its refracting visage
complimenting approaches
of barely knowable weather patterns
chameleon of technology
birthing countless hundreds of thousands
of micro-bio-nano bots built by hypocritical
tribes of silly little know-it-alls who enjoy symbolism
as much as any snake on a stick

Morphing
as per light & temperature,
sliding panel portals laser etched into broken
synaptic packages and a cool clean hep Hollywood/Philippines design
or the dirty plastic of vice verse ...
the entranceway is spacious
enough to accommodate
13 earth men
5' wide
{from shoulder to shoulder}
& 10' tall
{from head to toe}
If they'd all need to rush
out of or into the main chamber, all at once,
they could experience a slight claustrophobic thrill
with a bare minimum of inconvenience
No key is available, hence no key lost. The only method
of access is through your current intention. Though breach
has been accomplished {in earlier version 1.1 &2.0} the present
data mined of every tel-com transmit, be it terrestrial, celestial, or virtual
everyone with everyone of these examined through the Ecclesiastes Project,
funded all or in part by search engines, secret government agencies,
cellular carriers, old broken down CEOs, video sharers like yourself.
That's a 99 point floating nine success rate as per most recent
computations @this moment were these words to be read.

Only a blind architect could have coded this function

Every step you move forward the foundation moves
ever so slightly to the left [giving with gravity]
to compensate for the force of inertia.

"Hey, wait a minute here! What if five people move
in five different directions at once?"

What ... if ... The architect were not blind? Do you think this would be written?
Or a group of parser errors with extra content at the end,
what if you had to chew on that for a while with all your teeth
busted out OR if a {friendly} cracker was working
inside the corporation and THAT was the reason i lost that job?

Believe it or not,
i'm not smart enough to make this stuff up
the next wave pattern
of children leaping from prosperous loins
will be more
vicious than these
little birds in the fleshy palm

———◆————————————◆———

Pick up the Pieces

The horse is dead
don't beat it
their burgers are rotten
...don't eat it
wasteland preaches death & destructure
don't greet it
Love Light & Life
just be it
[[[In the last frame]]]
It could have been any color but yellow
yellow denotes mental instability in cinema
there she strolls—her hand lithely stroking the velvet rope
on the way back into—materia prima
smells of popcorn & Hollywood still linger
in this stale auditorium after opening night
The producer chuckles for no reason
"Yeah, that kid's got some kind of talent."
as he decides to pull the plug on the project

———◆————————————◆———

Chord Tangled Heart Word

Impossibility lends itself to the wonder of children
such is the mystery of love
which by all well-measured accounts
could not exist
on such a "perfect" world
full of superior people

Punctuate the Positive

Bleak lands call the hours to pasture
Creeping fungus gets involved in every
Crucial crevice and holds court in the time
It takes to look back
Even I send off this thought under the office
Of very low light in the land of unlimited
Electricity is at a premium
When these flood waters surge
Beauty is still
Everything & everything that is
Will & can be what it is
Beauty does not dwindle
Even though it crumbles
I'd like, one day, to wake
& truthfully bake
A wonderful creamy cake
Which'd have the power to slake
Even the most cruel cunning
Of the king of the world's stake
& banish all the human fake
In apocalyptic trenches of a worldwide
Cheesequake!
Silly. I know.
And seen has been believed
For the mind & soul of the creatures
Presumption in this paradigm of Me Time
Where the moments totter off
'Round mountain-sized stacks of products
& truth being held out of sight
While the keys to the pantry
Are passed off to the paltry
Rascals!
Varmints!
& their various offspring

Impending Woodpecker Doom

Whether it's rhythmic or not

you must keep knocking
hard upon this tiny spot
though t'would seem as a flaw
to all in the order of life
you must stand tall
or get swallowed
by the employees of glamor
who work in politic department
on the reform ticket
of the old guard

Whenever it rhymes
take a dip
be sure
the sun does not set
on your flourishings
nor dare the trapezistas
of the hyper-boreal
ever to be able
to buy you something
resembling lunch

Bailout the Downtrodden

Take from your trouser pocket
your stubborn fist
it would not help the people
to divvy up your lucre
Take from your shoulders
the ass sitting there
braying & eeyooring as stubborn as a man
lay down your yoke & plow
there is freedom waiting in the sound
let Love live;
shine that cosmic Light of Heaven

Permissible to Leave the Platform

will return
after thrusters & weights have been abandoned
3,000 frames a second is no cartoon
time folds in on space
radiating outward on spiraling arms
cosmic rooster
yolk of the galaxy
earth babies roll the bones
plucking petals like
there's no 2morrow

Curl the Wave

It bends to the will
inertial extra
she with the curls
flowing locks
makes the juggler
bend one knee
so he may offer
a wave emotive
from the depths
of a stony tome

◆—————————————◆

Sounds of Today

Hum the AC unit
Buzz the gnats
into the house
where live
a dog
&
a mouse
never enough time
but always a moment
for sounds
of peace

◆—————————————◆

Who's That Knocking?

That is the floor
This is my bed
Late night noises I hear
The sky is overhead

The walls stand firm
The Earth moves as she does
I go through the sunshine
With the bees and their buzz

The world will not end
Erase from your brain
Syllables of fear & hate
Eradicate the stain of pain

Hoping for peace; this world shall never end
Barking for war; our hearts will not mend
The glamorous life's corruption is a weight to be borne
Its brunt blunt grunt sings Sisyphus mourn

This is my bed
That is the floor
Please leave your well wishes
& flowers by the door

Whole Wide World

filled with people; their devices
break for the nautical palette
cool wind on white legs
primitive machinery
what could she say?
without transmission
silicon or rubber
the blubber of the well fed mass
they have decided to walk
their children on leashes
ITZA fashion
canine at least
this one over here
lovely as an unapproachable librarian
behind her glasses she dreams
of ballerina stretching
her leg hoisted up on the handrail
a ship coming into dock
an island of rock
their main industry
soft, recycled seagull figurines
like a seadoll
crafted by seagull
organic as seaweed
on full fathom dive
from out the inside
Atlantis returns to the land
i don't want anyone
gettin' too fruity
with this higher cerebral stuff ...

Twitching

This is a time to consult the rumbles of the stomach.
Night has come and gone again ...
All the clever realisticles have melted
In an epileptic puddle as the last lightning bolts
Picked up all their toys
Returning to the trailer park caverns
From whence they erupted
Not as long ago. Has another stooped to find
Has something the matter been?
Have birds their hearts boiled
Dropping into the gear housings
Of mud cakes with the right certification
Lovely? Where have you offed yourself to?
Just yesterday {was it not?} with dreams as technicolor
As cotton candy on a Ferris Wheel
And now, here, today ...
Only steel grey clouds masking the moon.

Blades clogged with wet grass

the sun has risen
a rooster headed Bostonian
squats in Terrier fashion
to the beat of a well-oiled machine

the sun has not yet begun
to char its flesh
what works these mama fields
before running them cool streets

the sun is on the one
whose eye is on this thick, wet grass
as a lover
lying in wait
to feel his whirring blade

Beware the Russian Room @Shakespeare & Co {Paris}

It is quite tight & hidden from prying
Secret eyes privately beckon
"Hey! Come over here & check this out!"
KGB nostalgia fr3aks & lovers
Of the poetry of Mother Russia
The space is so confined

Bent and packed against bohemian shelves
With all the Vladimirs & Natashas
All the Piotrs & Sonias
A veritable history of sexually charged,
Vodka fueled philosophics

Ripe for the plucking
A guilty secret
In subterfuge

———◆—————————◆———

Before Sunrise

A text book over-thinker thought for hours and hours
the perfect bytes, from pure essence, to relay
from her grandiose tower compound of scowers
scripted spidering devices released through cyber-info-hi-way

she gathered all the vegetables from all the corners of her town
built a database with AI remote-controlled infrared holograms
from the recesses of her toy chest, she pulled a threadbare clown
cross-scripted a channel of Dylan to crank out a few backmasked stereograms

At the end of the night
the whole thing went down
Hey-Ho, hot-cha-cha!
the whole thing went
down
down
down

◆—————————◆

Footage

To tie a cord in continuity
shoot the fish on a blue screen
Give him a sandwich
made of empty paper
before you roll the b-roll

Ten Shots Later

Jump through the frame
Rip a leg off
We can make it better in the edit
They'll want to point & click a bikini
on an island they've never seen
Vision is a tangibility
delicious in its suppleness
dainty in its decadence
memorable in its hypnosis

———◆———

Association of the Visceral

Stretch this day into your sleepy bones
hope last night you had your oxygen
there is a problem with terrestrial transmission
seashells mark our path to the end
Greet the animals with the Sun

be a sister or brother to every one
engage the visual aspects of the world
relax your mind in this cosmic swirl

———◆———

———————

Yesterday's Tomorrow

Kirk swaggers up
he grabs a space chick
stares deep into her eyes
"What's a doll like you doing in a Universe like this?"
He kisses her luscious purple lips
She morphs into an animate mound of lawn clippings
Kirk is disgusted
His science officer smirks silent
as he uploads the video to the chief engineer,
& the doctor, & Uhuru,
Who's laughing now James T?
Who's laughing now.

———————

The Day of Today

Doesn't the Earth seem more furious?
I know a guy who got stabbed in the shoulder
He's a skinny guy. A young man.
He gets paid to guard product
@a consumer warehouse on Independence Blvd.
the young lady didn't wish to be incarcerated
she pulled out a blade & shoved it through
the meatiest part
of this guy's torso
He's got a scar to prove it.

Streaming Through

Life is not your enemy
this road we travel was crafted
by every footstep before us ...
leads us to that place
we want to be

breathe

Love & be free
There aren't any shackles
to stop you from dancing
with all your heart
with all your soul

————◆————

Today's Fractal Is the World

The dog is going to the doctor
riding in a luxury sedan
flocks of angels descend
wishing peace & light
the chauffeur of the dog
is my chauffeur too
the path of the world
leaves a faint, perceptible trail
etched into all our retina
as we enter the clinic
across from the mall

◆————————◆

Plummeted From Heightened Insight

Run along these graveled streets
Ask a pension for your task
Fly through waves of watery wind
Leave a note of smoke in the den
Tell the conductor you lost your way
on staying awake for night and a day
Stretched to pull from Heaven's grasp
Run along these graveled streets

Morning Song

Early these birds do sing
of Life & bees
& wondrous scenes
sounding out the backyard
across the meadows' slumber
through the woods & over stream
they sing of sun & sea
to call us from our dream

———————

Earthsongs

Ramping up the production of expendable artillery
None seem to mind the quiet pains
of salad days spent in the garden
what could be paradise
were it not for the dark husks left
astride furrowed Earth
nor the pages of calendar
marked up in toxic slush

Earthsongs, as heard on high

———————

Observe Human

"That's what I said."
—after flicking pickles & pepperoncini off the stainless steel benches—
beneath the Morning Glory bells—STILL quite statefully perplexed
regarding this inability to boot that Plan9 .iso disk from the prompt—I
was told by God to take a walk—instead of tasks routinely performed
—also to record the day's 1st inkling of human word—Those words
[the first {coherent as human dialog} <in American English>] weren't
recorded until the southeast corner of Union Square—The next is a
mechanical recording from a sight-seeing bus—"This tour begins at the
corner of Geary & Powell, in Union Square."—Finally, an old, bald lady
comes to sit beneath this tree with me—She descends heavily upon
the pickley-mayoed concoction—She is protected by the thick
garment of her knee-length woolen peacoat—The Sun begins hotting
up—Early morning tourists scramble for the most perfect digital
photograph—"Are you looking at the pictures?"—trumpets one to
her gaggle—The old No. 8 {Hook & Ladder} sneaks through the
Square—spectators become visibly somber until it makes the light—
Seems, mainly from this observation, people refrain from
communication—unless, among themselves—The birds & automobiles
are constantly verbalizing—A mammoth of a fake laugh erupts from
the top of a double-decker bus—The rest are language sounds I am
unable to decipher—Whether for volume, regional dialect, or plain &
simple—"I just don't know."—The sound of this world is composed
through lyrical meter—The subtle nuance—best communicated to the
seeker—through the tranquility of observation—from a place peace
within the soul

—Sneak Thief Attacked by a Sea Snake—

Birdy, birdy bitch boo
a torpedo comes a-callin' with a kerchief
& a yoo-hoo!
& all the little fellers done left mama's nest
only to return on a forlorn & bleak future day

Wordy birdy snitch-a-poo
Whisper in the Ward "who done who?"
plus supernature inspiration mended on the wind
with a wig of a wam shuttled forth on the wing of a wlan
with a beady eyed beak face you'll meet your Thule

Malignant magpie of misfortune
can't you find the light?
Even @the brown cloak you must caw a fight
until that hopeful day; you will rule the world
Chick-cane! Chick-cane!
before the cats take over
& rip that chirp off your shoulder

Clutched From the Jaws of the Abyss

The sun is shining/rising to its apex, as the good people of the night before,
particularly reasoning, things beyond their control
—IT'S THE END OF ALL TIME!—
sales/sanitation/transportation are everything
everywhere you want to be
That's too late for you, boy-o.
Shoulda got outta here a wee bit earlier.

***

the first in a series of written & long-thought-forgotten
Mnemonic writings on the diverse subjects
As known by the peoples of the Barbary Coastal regions
during the reign of terrorist global dictators
& commercial-sponsored oil wars they inquiringly campaign for
being penned mainly in both local & public establishments
of the previously aforementioned location
By no known person of literary worth or merit
may it please the court, take note of this foray into quite proper grammar for
this too shall pass

***

In a terribly uncomfortable city
peopled by massively uncomfortable people
sitting in the sun
harboring resentment
including everybody else
everybody, that is, unlike
unwilling to be like their ideals
everyone who is outside their equations
mathematical co-rectitude
included in this population are the psycho
post-beatniks of golden hippie days

Who-za-wazoo happened way-way back before everything
went right-wing liberal progressive to say
"We are right and you are not."
Which is easy to see why it should be this way
every one of these yellow-livered peacocks wants to mate
with a peacock of equal or superior plumage

***

Long Australian shadows line the field radiating in from the East
This is only a micro-history
First the Spanish, next the French, Then the Asians, Americans, Irish, Maltese,
until finally the New Yorkers rolled up Nob Hill
planting a flag and resolutely stating "This is us!"

& the big question "Why?"
so this guy over here can chuckle madly as grace is sung at the opening of
Saturday night and the festivities this implies
The fashion & passion keeps pushing everyone further
go further the next great one is totally down the alley
around the corner, next week, or next year

***

I am surrounded and outnumbered
this could very well be my last bullet here in my palm
these books are starting to take over all the space in life
people will always tell you that people read
isn't true they don't read so much as to unmercifully crush
everything that is the writer's

***

Uniform Visitor Policy
Section 41D City Board of Supervisors passed the Uniform Visitor Policy for
Residential Hotels in 2002. This law prohibits all visitor and guest fees and
guarantees tenants the right to have visitors between 9:00am and 9:00pm, as well
as eight overnight guests per month. The Rent Board is charged with enforcing the
law along with the Police Department {Police Code Section 919.9}.

***

This morning when I open it,
The shower door, the little black underwear on the floor
and the roaches, we're rushing forward
as if they could somehow compose a virtual map

living crumpled with the "No Trespassing" sign
someone else crashed there last night
so I pulled out the back of the firescape,
and the roaches.
Ohh mama! They wanted
to carry the black underwear back
to the crack house
down the hall.
It was all switched flipping
~this meant a lot~

I had no idea what
I should do
I thought about it
For a few
& walked down the street
To a church

***

126

It doesn't sound like much
yet to be under the influence.
I'll be fully automated
just stream another summer sunset.
Please leave, still fresh with the obvious
insect again. Con convenience scene at once,
both on consequence y'all and I are time,
shudder at, how the total macNutt of all them.
I need. I saw on this, its entirety call around,
but I have more strike and subsequent
tackle all of these modern lumber traffic trolley
that is, if you're not into depressing minimalist
one of the ego to speak split ends
of self portrait cartoon characters
turn off all the invoices
see if it's possible
if you can without looking into this
is reflective surface of me. Order doors. Order Locks.
Order what we want
We needed ... it was more money
on the Bay Area and Nawlins if you can possibly
to reach a place Denny never ends
the fronts. Also palm that was stomped when evening
sellers call in the absurdly cramped hall,
"Hello, this is Lou."
& the multi-deadbolt door unscrews

celestial

the glass is never a half anything
Either is, or isn't
you soon spy the hall
watch the liquid get sold.
He's got the material considered. After All, Empty or full.
There is something that hurts everyone—all of us.
It's in millions of dollars and a telling.

***

***

Everybody has something
to say
about
everything
&
everything
has something
they say
to say
about everyone

***

The only ones I know to trust are: angels,
saints, & sometimes, priest {/ess/e/s}
After getting popped in the eye by a minor demon connected to the infiltration
horde of 2010 through a speed fr3ak /crack slinging demoniac of the St Moritz,
I was clutched from
the jaws of the Abyss, this time by this Saint of New Struggle Multi-Media & his

priestly brass-knuckled, bone-wagon driver
& that, Mr Frost, has made all the difference
In my small slice of world

***

This, from one circle, here: intown full of circles
Nothing is wasted.
Neither by the broken nor the destructors.
Holy objects are handled readily
Some caress them lovingly
others slap their meathooks all over 'em
in remembered ritual

***

There is a famous phrase:
"The souless are the godless
& the godless are
the dead & the dull."

Forgive me: It is a quite difficult quote to locate. I began its promoted usage in the mid-90s. I believe one appendage to this phrase {it should, at a future point, be stored as a cross-linked footnote}

Love is the food of the soul

You will notice the lack of quotation marks, no doubt.

***

Within the sanctuary of San Francisco's Saint Patrick's writing in this sacred place underneath the stained glass of/from Dublin, I, with all the Mothers & the green marbled pillars rising there also rises a faint & feeble strand of "Hallelujah!" I am CLUTCHED from the jaws of the Abyss by the same stone the stonemen rejected being flown, air-lifted along the road less traveled on the very narrowest path of this landfill via the celestial voices of angels
those you feel more than hear/
hear more than see/
yet, see: Everywhere/
in every gleam of Light.

***

The angels have arrived
Let the war begin
In the battlefield of love
I will defend you
'til the very end

***

Hello World

did my programming cause you
some sort of coughing jag?
Please don't mind the person writing in the silhouette of dusk...
it's only work
if you get paid for it.
Give my regards to
sincity,
vampiretown,
zombieville,
and all points out there
in the dark edge
of the world
with the telemetry backbeat
echoing long
frosty
mechanical
echoes.

PMPope is an American frontiersman and the first video poet of the turn of the century. A maverick in the fields of spoken word performance and the newly emerged field of digital artwork, it would be more than a decade before the world totally embraced the idea of a global cyber-social movement from the poetic vision. Today, PMPope is "in his element." Embracing the constant barrage of electronic media and hyperreactive communications, PMPope watches the event horizon with a keen interest in historic, current, and future events. Armed with an unending measure of indomitable hope and wild assortments of words and word by-product, PMPope sets his sights on transmitting poetry through the final frontier and beyond.

www.ingramcontent.com/pod-product-compliance
Lightning Source LLC
Chambersburg PA
CBHW051730090426
42738CB00010B/2189